INEFFABLE

INEFFABLE

Diving Into Outdated Thinking Patterns
And Embracing The Peace Within

CAITLIN LEIGH

SAT CHIT ANANDA

GRATITUDE
AND BLESSINGS

It is an honor to share this perception of reality with all Beings. There have been many roads traveled, and at this point, it is time to bask in the joy, beauty, and peace that simply is. Much love and blessings to all that is, for there are no words that can truly encapsulate the beauty and gratitude resting in the center. It is truly ineffable. Special thanks to Gabriella Novaky, John Mulligan, Linx Love, Jamie Francis, Diane Pfister, Conni Renee, Amy Burns, Joshua Rivers, Susan Bond, and Stecie April for your loving support in bringing this beautiful book blessing into fruition. Your support is a divine gift and blessing. Love, joy, and peace to all Beloveds.

A river of reverence stretches my heart
into the vastness of the ineffable; here you
and I drift away, dancing as One.

AUTHOR'S PERSPECTIVE

And within a blink of an eye, my life had changed. That once joyous, smiling, loving, exuberant child was locked into a closet. It is as if neurons in my brain had something else in mind for me at age 13. From that day on, there was a one-pointed focus on all of life's distractions. Give me more. More, more and more. And for me this manifested through the body in an outward form. My life goal was to become as thin as possible, invisible, as it were. And so the journey began.

Wake up and weigh myself. Depending on what I weighed, go eat a little. Drink some water, go weigh myself. Go to school, think about how to lose weight. Go home.... weigh myself. Get ready for volleyball, weigh myself. Eat some dinner, and then weigh myself. Go to volleyball, come home and weigh myself. Drink some more, weigh myself again. Weighing myself sometimes 30 times a day. The eating became less and less, and the weighing became more and more. An endless cycle. And out of this innocence such a habit was created. And others too. The weighing never stopped. But the purging began. And then the drinking. And then the pills. And the cutting. And then the binging. And the negative thoughts. And the multiple psych hospitals. And the codependent relationships. And the isolation. And then the relapse. And a final surrender. And within a blink of an eye, my life would change forever. It is as if something within knew. That there was more than this, more possibilities. A trinkle of faith. And this became a slow surrender. Every day, bit by bit, a slow surrender. Losing grip of all the programming I held onto from such innocence. For it is all in innocence. I used to wake up and ask myself, "What is wrong with me? There must be something wrong." And this slowly transitioned into wanting to end my life. And this slowly transitioned into me admitting I needed help. And this transitioned into, "Everything will be ok." And this slowly transitioned into, "I have the power to choose." And this transitioned into loving kind affirmations of the self. And this transitioned into loving acceptance of all this. And this transitioned into, "Life is beautiful... all is perfect." And this transferred into an eternal state of joy, serenity, bliss, and peace. And I have realized that this whole journey was not out of some deep karmic cycle or punishment from God, but a gift to consciousness itself. For in the process, I have learned the mind is like a toddler; it is pure innocence. We are all innocent, and out of our innocence we become programmed. And when we decide to take a step outside of the programming, and surrender to the infinite Presence, miracles happen. In fact, life is a continuous miracle. This journey was a gift of Presence, teaching me that we are all powerful. We all have a choice. We are all love. God lives within us all. We are all one choice away from seeing this miracle that is life. And in this state of surrender, eternal serenity arises. I was given this experience to share that anything is possible in the realm of consciousness. We have a choice. The power resides within...no need to look without. Blessings, Beloveds.

It is an utterly and overwhelming space to be in when the thinking fritters away, and one is consumed by the all-pervading infinite love. Incapacitating. What was, is no longer; what is, simply is. It is perfect. Absolutely exquisite. For there are no bounds in which to collide. Floating in an eternal void of peace. The state of omnipresence. Omnipotence. All judgements have relinquished. The perception of time and space have dissolved, and one has yielded to the Presence; the totality of all that is. Beyond what any mind could ever conceive. Beyond the beyond. Isness. Here, basks eternity. The "I Am" presence. All desires and wants cease. There is no getting or gaining. There is simply Presence. And this, itself, Complete. Bask in this completeness, for it is not somewhere "out there", but simply right here, in this continuous moment. May all be blessed by the unbridled joy that unfurls in the here and now.

—Welcome

Trust the divinity
Of "Self"
For it is there
Every
Step
Of the way
Whispering
Its sweet nothings
Of love and kindness.

—Holding Hands

Ecstasy
Is the dance
Between
The unfurling mind
And
Emptiness.

—Here

So tired
Laying it down
Laying it all down
Every bit of it
At the feet of
God
Surrendering
To
One mind.

—Relief

For one that
Is not ready to
-Hear-
The truth
Will sound
Like blasphemy
-Pause-
The truth
Is ever present.

—Readiness

There are sorrows that run so deep, it leaves one breathless. There is grief so unutterable, the heart seems to escape the chest. There is pain so poignant, one will never be the same. There is a despair so palpable, joy is choked down with a heavy sigh. There is an omnipresent mourning, where all collectively weep for a savior. There is suffering so ubiquitous, beauty showers over with its stillness and grace. And there is a peace so ineffable, God arises within all. And the light of lights, divinity beams through every waking heart with a glimmer of infinite love and gratitude.

—Heal

The release
Of conceptual
Thinking
Allows
A sort of
Freedom
That is beyond
A temporary
Pleasure
Sought out
By the seeking
Mind.

—Nonlinear

God said
Keep those hands
Open
For there is
An endless
Well of love
Surrounding
And always
Awaiting
A welcome
Home.

—Faith

This all-pervading glory of goodness
shines its love for all that is.

—Available

The eloquence of consciousness is an ever expansive Presence evolving into infinite potentialities. It is the absence of the finite, and presence of Absolute. This all-encompassing Presence is continuous, extraordinary in its blossoming, subtle in its evolution. Shifting. Pulsating. Being. Consciousness is an ungraspable phenomenon, that is sought to be grasped by the grappling mind. Yet is ungraspable. Unthinkable. Unknowable. And the mind seeks to know, but the mind can only know about. It is limited. Consciousness, unlimited. Play it safe, the mind says. Bring reason and logic into everything. Prove this, prove that. See, the mind plays small. For its scope is only a fraction of the totality of existence. Its perceiving. Its projecting. All stem from its limited awareness. Its yearning to define the undefinable. Its yearning for safety. To put it all in a box. Then what. Remove the box, this is consciousness. The mind is enveloped in this all-pervading infinite bliss. Consciousness. That box is illusionary. Created by the thinking mind. It is not real. For the truth rests in infiniteness, boundlessness. Existence, consciousness, bliss. The mind is so innocent, it continues to seek for its safety. For consciousness' destiny is to return to its source. And when the mind returns to its very source, there will be no such thinkingness. Only beingness. Bliss. Peace. Presence.

—Pretty Little Box

In deep
Search of
Truth
All
Is revealed.

—Devotion

God's radiance
Glistens as the blissful void
Of goodness
Omnipresent
Omnipotent
God is everywhere
No space or time
Blessed is all
For all is
Kissed
By the infinite love
Of God.

—Subjectivity

The glistening waters
Dance with
The vibrant sun
Interconnected
Euphorically
Emitting
A gleam
Of
Divinity.

—Beautiful

Blissful bliss
Soaking in
The magnificence
That is
A joy so loud
Existence
Dances
In laughter.

—Humor

Lighten the grip
Relax in the
Loving light
Of gleeful
Serenity
Breathe
The precious
Gift
Of tranquility
The presence
Of God
Blesses
All
That welcome
And continues
To bless
When unwelcome
The omniscience
Of God
Is a wonderous
Delight.

—Blessings

Shake shake shake
Laugh laugh laugh
Smile smile smile
Dance dance dance
Be be be
Embrace the
Simplicity
Of divinity.

—Take One Moment

Allow the brilliance of
This moment
To kiss
The wandering
Mind with
Stillness
And watch it
Rest
In a peaceful calm
Surrendering
It empties
Into the now
No longer grasping
Embracing
All BEing.

—Silence

Traverse through
Boundlessness
Igniting the fire
Of illumination
Break through
Any limits
That have been
Perceived by the
Mind and -release-
Enter the
State of
Awareness
Singing the song
Of peace
One may
Simply
Be.

—Now

Fading into the stillness of the now. Washing away resistance. Sinking into the boundlessness. Breathing in as All. And right here, is it. The unfurling mind has lost its grip. Without edges, it becomes one with the permeable existence. The eternal Presence. Right here, is it. Settle into the bliss of infiniteness. Settle into this gentle stillness living within. Allow it. Welcome it. Bask in it. A miraculous delight, to return to this Presence. And when there are moments that seem like too much, come back to here. Right here, is it. For God is always here. In this moment. So, when it all seems too much, just come back right here. This eternal Presence is always here. Within. Waiting for all to return. For all to remember All is All. And that God is not "out there" but right here. Within. Breathing through All. Right here, is it. Rest in this, beloved.

—Right Here

Shimmering shining stillness
A solitude
Of purity
One soaks in
The glory
Of God
Breathing
In all that
Is.

—Nature

The moon
Kisses the stars
Each night
With its
Nurturing glow
The evening
Is lit up
With a silent
Glee
All sleeps
Heavenly
In this
Divine abode
Infinitely.

—Awakening

There is a radiance
To all that is
When one
Allows oneself
To truly see
Freeing all
Those tightly
Held attachments
Of comfort
Into the vast sea
With nothing
To grip
One floats amongst
A boundless ocean
Of love, joy, and peace
What serendipitous
Space to
BE.

—Surrendering

Quiet the mind
In its rapacious
Desire to think
Think
Think
Think
The thinking never stops
One might say
Slow down
Slow it all the way
Down
Breathe in
The stillness
Of this very moment
And watch
The deceptions
Of mind
Dissipate
Into the
Field of
Nothingness
Emerging
A silent
Elation
For this
Is simply
Consciousness.

—Be

Relish in the splendor
Of Allness
Dissolving
Into infinite love
Basking in the
Glory of eternity
The emergence
Of bliss
From a simple
Surrendering
To the totality
Of Being
Give it up
And swim
In the divinity
Of omnipresence.

—Infallible

In a constant state of surrender, one is led to its Destiny. For in surrender, there is a gentle unraveling of the mind. And in this unraveling, miracles are revealed. For miracles are blooming in Presence. Resistances start to fade away, and the seeking slows to a halt. And when the seeking stops, the mind becomes steady in the stillness. Sigh. It pauses in the Peace. This is the eternal now. Surrender. For All is yearning to return to its source. Surrender. It is the destiny of consciousness to return to its source. Surrender. This is the letting go of suffering. Surrender. This path is available to All, for All is free. Surrender, beloved. There is infinite bliss in simply Being.

—Pause

The beauty of
This moment
Is nameless
For it transcends
All limits
That have been
Conceived from
The mind
In its illusionary
Holding onto
Of what is
Not
For there
Is nothing
Absolutely nothing
That may be
Held
In voidness
Allness.

—Free

Weaving through
The silky softness
With a gentleness
A tender humility
Smile so heavenly
Showering in the grace
Of a merciful
Eternity.

—Still

Kissed with love
Seen in light
Beloveds do not
Worry
For all is well
Blessings
Shine
The
Infinite bright
Light.

—Relax

If it brings peace
By all means
Shower it with
A golden yes
And if it brings
Anything outside
Of peace
One may
Ask
What for?

—Self-Inquiry

Sometimes it
Is inevitable
To not be washed
Away from the
Piercing waves
Of sorrow
Striking the
Deepest core
-Dear one-
This is the moment
To allow
Divinity to
Shine forth through
The suffering
Of all that is
Allowing grace
To stretch its
Wings and wrap
The Beloved
In a warm
Embrace.

—Kiss

Many misconceptions
Arising from the
Thinking mind
To cling to outdated
Projections so
As to serve
An illusionary
Survival
-Pause-
There is nothing
To survive
When all
Is
"It."

—Projections

Share the gift of God through understanding. Gently letting go of control, for such is an illusion created by the mind. It becomes so cyclical, surrender is feared. And pride is clung to in hopes to repress what is sifting below the surface, while humility is only one choice away. There is a gentle crumbling from what was to shine forth what truly is. Undoing what has been done. Humility is only one choice away. Freedom awaits all that submit to losing grip of a fallacious identity. Stripping away every untruth. And allowing truth to disperse its eternal Presence into all that is. It can be a struggle, and yet it can also be truly simple. Softly, let go. Let be. Surrender to the ubiquitous beauty when one jumps into boundless understanding.

—The Pathway of Surrender

The stillness
Offers an eternal
Peace that
Welcomes
All that is
With non-attachment
And within this
Love blooms
Effortlessly
In boundlessness.

—Eternity

It is impossible
To lose
Anything or Anyone
For All
Is the
One.

—Attachment

There is no rush
Or hurry
-Beloveds-
For there
Is a boundless
Tolerance
Within the
Presence
Absent of time
Or space
It waits patiently
And joyously
For All
To remember
The essence
Of All that is
Home
That of the
Supreme Spirit.

—In Divine Timing

An insatiable doubt continues to arise. Every. Step. Toward. Surrender. Dragging feet. Slowly. Softly. But what if this. And what if that. The mind continues to ponder the next step. Anticipating the future. Projecting its fears to protect its sweet angelic fragility. Holding itself together. As if it were not meant to be boundlessly open. Free. Beautiful doubt. A guide toward one's ultimate freedom. And sweetest surrender. For each time doubt arrives, in that moment one let's go just a little bit more. And then a little bit more. And then a little bit. More. For when doubt visits, welcome it as a loving child of God and ask what it so desperately seeks, but is unsure it will find. Go ahead. It is there. The answer is, without a doubt, within.

—Teacher

Looking around, one sees deception, pain, and the suffering of the world. Curling up in a ball, hiding. Trying to rid oneself of these untruths. The deception. The lies. And this can be too much. Take a deep breath. And ask what does holding on to this do? What for? Here is where the unraveling of the "lies" begins. Where one starts to make amends with the deceit the world has thrust upon them. Where accountability is taken for one's life. Where one starts to release the conditioning. Where one starts to lose grip on all the transitory attachments. Where one realizes, the truth has been there all along in its all-pervading Presence. Where one has the choice. The power. The love. To choose all that is in Truth. May the truth in All be revealed.

—Beautiful Deception

Once one tastes
The truth
Infinite possibilities
Shine through
Clearing
Mind derived
Attachments
Faith sifting below
The surface
As one prays
To God
To reveal
The inner strength
So as to embody
The love
Of God.

—Revelation

Sitting with those noisy neighbors. Those funny things called thoughts. That just never seem to stop. And some of them seem oddly true, but some of them are downright retched. But all of them, if anything, are simply just thoughts. Nothing more, nothing less. And sometimes those thoughts come to life. And sometimes those thoughts are shoved deep inside. But all thoughts are in the love of God. For every thought that is thought, love is always there. And it could be the most retched thought, the scariest and most frightful destructive thought. Yet God is right there. In this thinkingness, this all-pervading love is right there. So, the neighbors may be noisy, but remember home is where the love is. And it is holding the space. And when it gets too loud, it is ok to simply just Be.

—Loving Mind

Planning for a perfect tomorrow. Wor
what it may bring. Thinking it over, thinki
way through. Ruminating. The anxiety bui
to create this perfect tomorrow. A day that has yet to arrive, but is so occupied by the mind. To stay busy. To fill. Keep going. So, the mind keeps going. Filling in all the blanks. Thinking about a tomorrow that has not arrived. Making plans for an illusionary day, moment. Time is passing by and the mind is engulfed with the perfection of tomorrow. And the next day. And, the next day. And the following. It goes on. And on. And on. Thinking and thinking about all the possibilities of an imaginary future. Pondering, planning, escaping, avoiding, filling the present moment with the anxiety of what is not real. And that is what the mind will do. Fixate on all those imaginations, prioritizing such illusions over the present moment. For what? Preparing for another day, when all there is, is this moment. Breathe, and simply drop all of that. Drop tomorrow. Drop the planning. Drop the projections. And simply breathe the breath of this beautiful moment. Surrender to now. Sigh in relief, in the exquisiteness of this Eternal Now. For God is right here. God is not tomorrow. Or the next day. God is in the nowness of this very moment. Presence, is all that is asked. So, allow the mind to be at rest just for this moment. Just for one moment, be with God. Just for one moment, breathe in the love that is All. For All is love, and All is God. And God is right here, now. In this very moment.

—Simple Request

43

The experience
Becomes an exquisite
Paradise
Promising
Ineffable beauty
In its
Complete
Presence
-Take a leap-
Boundlessness
Will carry
All home
To the Allness
That is.

—Togetherness

This is the moment of moments. The grandest of them all. This eternal moment is a forever now. And the beauty of this nowness, is an unshakeable Presence. Timelessness. And this moment continues. It is unending. Infinite. And there is such splendor in this Presence. Oneness. And from this totality springs forth a boundless gladness. Ripples and ripples of gladness. It is an infinite joyous celebration of completeness. Basking in wholeness. The everlasting innocence shines forth. Presence is a fertile ground for all that is pure. And All is pure, and All is encompassed by this Presence. So be, darling. Just be. Swim in beautiful eternity. Gladly.

—Lovingly

Sometimes in that hollow space of loneliness. The pit of isolation. One touches the depth of depths. Intensely. For some, it is too much. This depth is within All. And when this depth is greeted with a tenderness, like that of a child, within this spacious awareness it simply becomes an infinite Presence. One realizes this depth is simply an unbounded state of being. Where one has surpassed any limits, and all resistances have dissolved. And the Absolute is revealed. Totality. Self. Here, in this moment. Bask in the loneliness, welcome solitude. For in the emptiness, one will bask in the presence of God and bask in the infinite light of light.

—Empty

Every moment becomes one of opportunity. One of surrender. Complete surrender to all that is. For it is a chance, to give it up. Let it all go. Lay it all down. Completely. What is weighing on the heart, the mind, the spirit. Give it up. And let God. Sink into the steadiness of stillness. Be with God. As God. As this Presence. As All. For this is the truth. Be brave enough to let it all go and watch the miraculous-ness of this moment spill into eternity. Bliss. Ineffable joy. And shine like the effervescent loving sun.

—Infinite Light

There is a thing for this. There is a thing for that. There is a thing to fix this. And a thing to fill that. So many things. Infinite things. Focusing on the things. One pointed-ness on things. Collecting things. Grasping for things. Holding on to things. Perfecting things. Changing things. Distracted by things. Oh, so many things. The mind loves these things. For the mind loves form. And what happens when one stops feeding the mind these things? Welcome to the realm of formlessness, where now is an eternal state of being. One miraculous moment of radiant bliss.

—Things

From formlessness to form, words spill from the pen to paper. These words bloom from a surrendering heart, aching for the truth. These words do not come from the mind, for the mind cannot grasp what is being written. For what is being written is not graspable. How beautiful. What is being written is beyond. And it is right here. The lovely paradox that is life. The mind has lost it. It can no longer sink its claws into untruths, for the heart has touched it so lightly with its loving kindness. And that is the power of love. It is so soft. Subtle. Without intention or motive. And out of this innocence, it heals. This is love. Love, loves as love. There is no getting with love. This is the innocence of love, for it loves as love simply being love. Watch the mind sink into an open state when enveloped by this boundless love. Let the power of love rinse through the reaching mind, and watch it let go. Watch it float into the eternal moment of now. Presence, and peace.

—Newborn Words

Disintegration follows
As one continues
To question the adopted
Beliefs, perceptions, projections
Opinions and judgements
That continuously arise
Within the mind
-Poke, poke, poke-
For it is the perfect
Time to ask
Where did such thoughts
Come from
And what would
Happen if such
Thoughts, opinions, beliefs,
Perceptions, projections,
And judgements
Were released
-Just like that-
What then?

—For What

Understanding is a
Beautiful gift of
God that is
Present in All
It emanates its
Merciful love
Within this
Very moment
And it is
Only one
Choice
Away.

—Choice

And it all can be so funny. Projecting onto life what ought to happen. What it ought to look like. What one ought to see. To experience. To feel. Perceiving what is right. What is wrong. Defining what is good. What is bad. Trying to fit it all in a box. And not step outside of that box. For if one steps outside the box, all control is lost. And then what. Then what. Love can permeate All. Love can sift throughout the All. Love can move freely. Gracefully. For love does not belong in a box. Love does not project a type of thingness out into the world. Life. All. Love simply goes about being love. Loving. And if one tries to put love inside a box, one starts to experience the deception. The fallacy, that love ought to be a certain way. That love is a certain thingness. That loves like this. Feels like that. Acts like this. For this is a projection of the mind. The love that is being written about, cannot be perceived or felt by the mind. See, love is the essence. It is at the core of All that is. It is the truth of every Being. And no being belongs inside a box. For this boundless love loves infinitely and on without discernment. It simply loves, for it is love. Step outside of the box, and jump into love. Be, as love. For All is love.

—Jumping In

All is saturated with infinite
Benevolence
-Innocence-
For all is an emanation
Of the Divine
As one becomes cognizant
Of such divinity
Within
One expands into
All that is
Embracing the infinitude
Of Existence
And it will be
Likened to a warm
Welcome hug home.

—Hug

Sweet serendipitous moment of solitude. A moment saturated in benevolence. The innocence of all that is. Wrapped in a cocoon, yet marvelously connected. Sitting in this, relishing in this. Out of this cocoon, blooms a beautiful bliss permeating all of existence. There is no longer a this and that. Emerged from the cocoon is this and that. One is All. Out of the tightly held protective layers. The interwoven beliefs, projections, perceptions, and opinions. The entitled judgements. All untangling, loosening, and softening. Melting into all that is. Sweet loving solitude. The moment where one has reconciled with giving up, giving in. And basking in the humility of such. Sweet tender humility is the juice of innocence, softening every ridged heart and bringing it back to the purity that is. For all is pure. All is perfect. All is divine. Sweet joyous solitude, the taste of peace is wonderous and at the core of All. Look within, beloved. Enjoy the solitude.

—Within

Shimmering shades of softness
Cascade through the grace
Filled sky
Enveloped by a touch
Of serendipity
And blissful awakening
Blessed miracles fall
From the milky blue
Clear as day
All is well
The reminiscence are
Fading silently away
And as the sun vivaciously
Shines through
All is left
All are kissed
With a vibrant
Twinkle.

—Happy Day

When asking where is the mind, one will point to the head. As if the thought was derived from the head. As if the mind lived in the head. But where truly does the mind reside. When there is a cessation of thinkingness, then what. The mind that fills this void, this silent bliss. Is also the mind that completely unfolds into utter bliss. So where is the mind. Where does such thinkingness come from. The mind is encapsulated by this all-encompassing Presence. The universal mind. Consciousness. Existence. Brahman. The cessation of thinkingness allows the truth to reveal itself. As God manifest. As All that is. As Totality. As Consciousness. So, pause in the thought, surrender the mind to the One mind. Universal mind. And be washed away by the connectedness of all that is. The eternal bliss of now.

—Let Go

Laughter is truly a medicine of Existence. It is the gift of simply Being. For in laughter, one is able to shake off the seriousness of life. To dust off the distractions with lightness, and embrace life with grace and joy. The joy of being. Laughter has the most beautiful gift in penetrating to the core of all that is, and bringing out the innocence in one. Returning one to innocence. For this is what all is inherently. Laughter cuts through the minds pervasive thinkingness, and allows one to sink into the stillness. The quietness, and uncontainable joy beating within. As the mind begins to unwind, there is less holding to things. And the less holding to things, and the more laughing at things. Laughing just because. Laughing at the nature of life. The infinite paradoxes. Laughing, for there is nothing really one needs to do. So, laugh it off. Allow the resistance to be washed away by the grace of laugher and be enveloped by the infinite bliss of the Presence. Laugh, beloved.

—Medicine

And as one surrenders the seeking. As one surrenders the reaching's of the mind. As one lets go of the way things ought to be according to mind. As one surrenders all hopes and dreams. As one gives up on doing it all. As one releases the need to be right. As one kneels down in the face of struggle and adversity. As one surrenders the need to fix or correct. All can simply be. All can be exactly as is. And all can be embraced as is. All can be accepted and loved exactly as is. What a relief. The reins have been lifted. Control takes a step back. Anxiety is brushed with a stroke of gentleness. The mind letting go into the All. Fading into the All. Trusting in the All. Giving it up to All. For the mind can only go so far. It can only reach, and then it has its breaking point. Break. Please break. Crumble. For in the crumbling, the truth will be revealed. And the mind will pause, surrendering to this ineffable truth. This truth living within the All. As the All. Do not be afraid to crumble. To fall apart. To break down, as if the heart were to spill out of one's chest. It is ok. It is ok. There is great healing in surrender. There is great healing in humility. There are beautiful gifts waiting on the other side of that break. Go ahead, beloved. There is infinite strength within. Go ahead, and crumble. Fall apart. Break. Give it up to God. And breathe in the truth. The Perfection within, and without.

—Crumble

Leaning into joy
As a pillar of
Unbridled strength
And serenity
Dipping toes into
The infinitude
And melting into
The miracles
Blossoming
In the eternal
Now
-Breathe-
There is a global
Awakening happening
And All plays a role
In this blissful
Shift.

—Watch

And sometimes the very thing that is run away from, is the very thing that brings one back home to God. Within. The pain that is so often avoided through various distractions and infinite pleasures, holds the very key. The key to the miraculous, the infinite, the healing, the bliss. Pain is the doorway to the Divine living within. It is a gift from Self to self. When the chasing after pleasures subsides, and the pain is allowed to sink in, one is able to hear the whispers of God. One cries out for help, and the Divine answers. One can hear. Worldly matters shift, as the Divine within gets louder and louder. The material starts to dissolve, and what seems real is no longer real. And what seems unreal is awakened to as the truth. Sit with the pain, let it become a garden of unbridled truth ready to break through old paradigms and patterns. Sit with the pain, and watch as the suffering melts away. The truth is revealed, and All are awakened to the light shining within. Sit with pain, and let it speak to the Divinity within, and watch as the miraculous unfolds as a steady stream of consciousness.

—The Gift

Quivers of fear ringing
In the ear
Whispering of nothing's
And not yet to be's
A little shaky
One may be
Back to the heart
The quiescent infinitude
Rattling within
It whispers of no
Such things
For It is all of it
And beyond
Simply complete.

—Centering

Unbounded delight weaves seamlessly through the permeable edges of existence, bliss floats gallantly as a radiant wave of unwavering Beingness. Here is the home of the Heart. Here is what all go looking for, yet beats so effortlessly within. Here, Eternity.

—Tuning In

Life is a boundless opportunity
A spiritual playground
For transcending the limitations
Of the mind
Surpassing all the projections
And perceptions
Stretching past limitation
Into the realm of
Nonlinear
Into the power
Of emanation
For there is
Infinite power
Resting within
As all limitations
Are surrendered
And one is
Free to be
As the All
God is
Immanent.

—Breathe In

Ubiquitous miracles
Infinite beauty
Abundant love
Divine perfection
Radiant light
Unbounded joy
Radical authenticity
Liberated heart
Serenity becomes
All that is
And all that is
Becomes serenity
A blissful state
Of now
Fully immersed
In the now
A peace so still
All are
Awakened
To the perfection
Beating within.

—Transcending Distraction

Let the silent
Whispers
Of Divinity
Breathe through
Stillness
Reverberating
Through the
Emptiness
Of mind.

—Wake

.

It has been found
That when one
Has relinquished
Its attachments
Surrendering
All delights
The doorway
To heaven
Shimmers
In gladness.

—Patiently

When the busy-ness all stops. When the thinkingness winds down. The hustle and bustle comes to a halt. The distractions disappear. The desires fizzle out. The seeking fades away. The resistances dissolve. And everything that was held so tightly, let go. And the programming, is unprogrammed. And one returns to the innocence that is inherent in All. Lay those fears and delusions on a bed of roses and watch the Presence envelop All with a subtle all-pervading peace. All is taken over by a sweet serenity. The still mind is one of emptiness. A still mind has completely surrendered to Existence. A still mind, is one of complete innocence. Let the mind be still, this is where the miracles are. This is where the truth is revealed. For when the mind unfurls, the programming dissolves, and the truth that has always been there is received with deep reverence. And a bliss washes over, and one basks in an eternal state of Oneness. Still the mind, let it be still.

—Shhhh

The power of truth cannot be denied. For all that is power is love, and love has the power to dissolve anything that is not of truth. What is not true, makes one go weak. What is in truth goes strong. Love is power, and power is strength. And this infinite strength is ubiquitous. It is pervasive. It is in this very moment. This Presence. Unstoppable. It has the ability to heal all that is. And this is the power of power. It requires nothing outside of itself. It is total. Complete of its own. Complete.

—Powerful

Consciousness is complete in itself. It is perfect. And when one relinquishes the grip of the mind's projections, the fog clears. Clarity arises, and humility sinks in allowing one to bask in that utter silence. Stillness, known as Presence. Out of this Presence, one is emerged in an eternal peace. The eternal nowness. That is all perfect and beautiful. God has been revealed. God has been there all along. In this very moment. For God is right here. Not out there. But right here. And the heart expands out of its constriction, allowing the eternal peace to take over. Allowing the Self to shine through. The little "me" dissolves in this infinite space, and Self is ever present. Self as God. Self as Presence. Self as Existence. Self as All.

—Clarity

Humility trickles
Through the boundless
Energy of selflessness
Joyously Being
As one with all
As its rhythmic pulse
Shines through
The brilliance
Of all that is
Settling into a
Dance with
Infinitude
What a joyous
Bliss.

—Love

The sun shines forth
On all that is
It does not
Hide its spark
Because of
Something
It simply
Radiates its
Golden waves
As it is
And this is
Love
For love goes
On being as
Love
For it does
Not need to
"Do" anything
It simply
Needs to
Be.

—Authentic

Thus, is not captivated by this or that. Thus, is simply just that. Thus, is unknowing of any distractions, for it simply is as there are no distractions, longings, yearnings, or seeking for thus. What does one seek? Being, one surrenders openly to the path of God. The path of love. The path of releasing attachments, distractions, and yearning. Seeking is merely a trance, an illusion that there is something out there to reach for. And when that seeking is surrendered, an infallible joy is revealed. There is God.

—Strength

Equanimity
Blissfully rests
In the presence
Of Presence.

—Smile

Sometimes it gets
A little quiet
In this stillness
Quivers of joy
Radiate through
Being
And bliss
Dances along
For the ride
Of solitude
As the quietness
Sifts through
All that is
Leaving a remarkable
Silence
Emptiness
Now.

—Breath

Spontaneously
Questioning
The curiosities
That fill the
Infinite
Universe
Of isness
Wondering
But not reaching
Laughing
But not seeking
For all
Is already known.

—God

Shine light. Be light. Embrace love. Embrace light. All the barriers, blocks, resistances dissolve in the face of love, for love seeks to embrace all. The ineffable. Ease the suffering, so as to bring forth harmony for this is being. All is harmonious, all is well, all is healthy, all is whole. When was this forgotten? There are books with answers. There are teachings with plenty of guidance. There are gurus, one may listen. But truly, all answers are found within. Sit in the stillness. Bask. And in this stillness, one is awakened to the infiniteness. The boundlessness. The ineffability that simply is.

—Creator

One may
Get swept up
By the content
-Take a step back-
Allow context
To reveal
The truth
Of love
That dissolves
The linear mind
Softening
Its fearful
Grip.

—Trust In a Higher Plan

Consciousness is a magnificent masterpiece
Transcending all time and space
Enveloping all that is
The return home
Will be one
Of bliss.

—Unification

Time is merged as an eternal now. And all form ceases, dropping into formlessness. The edges have softened into a permeable existence. And All is enveloped by this infinite Presence. In this state of Being, there is an ineffable joy for the ego has lost its grip. Fully surrendered to Self. Self is revealed, and one now has a taste of Completeness. Divinity. Basking in this eternal Completeness. It is not a feeling, nor a thought, it is simply a way of being. The essence of Presence, God. Surrendering all that is false, one is only left to dance in the truth. That which is the essence of simply Being. Love, joy, serenity. Peace. And how beautiful. To humbly let go, of all that is holding one back from remembering the Presence that is All. All is All. And God is the eternal now shining through the infinite light of All.

—Freedom

Shimmering golden light
Wrapped around the earth
The warm embrace
Of love
Glistens
As the light continues
To grow
-Glow-
The all encompassing
Presence of love
Amplifies
And all beings
Gather
To go home.

—Brahman

Take a sip
Of the Presence
It is the
Limitless
Nectar of life.

—Omniscience

Send loving kindness within
Without
Extend compassion for
All that is
Share the infallible joy
Resting
In the heart
And bask in the
Balance of
Life.

—Sublime States

The only moment is here and now, and it is truly a sublime moment. Not to experience, but recognize one is it. One is all of it. One enters a deep state of ineffability as it basks in the continuation of all that is, consciousness. Separation, illusionary. One is it! Celebrate the infiniteness that arises from BEing.

—Existence

Ineffable blessings
Blossom out
Of the Presence
A mighty
Stillness
Sings its peace
In the quietness
Basks
An unfettered
Joy
With a luminous
Glint
Sprinkling
Drops of
Laughter
For this is
The power
Of love.

—Miracles

Blessing all with
A touch of joy
Magnificence
Is within all
For all is divine
All is perfect
All is beautiful
All is.

—Is

Softly it goes a little something like this; crack, crack, crack. Alert, CONSTRICT. A gentle opening arises within. Crack, crack, crack. CONSTRICT. Opening further, gently nudging one toward the open doorway, the Presence. All that is; merciful, forgiving, loving, joyous. It is true. It awaits the surrendering. Hesitation. Do not know. Letting go. A quiet stillness brings forth the yearning for all that is. The Presence, boundlessly open, awaits. Greets all with an overwhelming peace. Crack, crack, CRACK. One arrives in a splendid state of limitlessness. A state of peace. One has become the Presence. For all is enveloped by the beloved Presence. All is welcome. Eternally.

—Boundlessness

May all receive
The bountiful
Beauty
Brimming
At the center
Of the
Heart.

—Presence

Smoothly sailing through the unknown. All fear and worry has drifted away, and love simply permeates all that is. What was once a struggle is now embraced with a loving acceptance. A deep reverence, as though it is perfect. For whatever is, is perfect. It is All perfect. So if the sun shines today, how lovely. And if the sun does not shine today, how lovely. It is as if the world could be on fire, and that would be just beautiful, perfect. For whatever is burning on the inside, will be mirrored outside. And in this moment, everything is simply perfect. For the "I Am" has been embraced. And this feeling of completeness has taken over. Totally absorbed in one's wholeness. What is felt inwardly, is reflected outwardly. And everything is so darn beautiful. Remarkable. The beauty is magnificent, and perfect. Basking in this wholeness, dancing in the completeness. A beautiful world is reflected back to all that is Complete. This innocence is found in All.

—It's There

One may go searching for it. Reaching for it. Praying for it. But this may be a cyclical task. For "it" is not something to be gained. "It" is not something out there. Lay down all teachings. Lay down all reaching. Lay down all the beliefs. Lay down that tight grip. For truth is of the formless. God is beyond all form and rests in the Presence of all that is. To surrender this cycle of searching for "God" or enlightenment will allow the ultimate to shine forth as truth. This is it. Bask in the miracles. Breathe in the completeness, Beloved. All is Complete.

—Wholeness

One has arrived
In the state
Of boundlessness
Where duality
Is laughable
No beginning
Nor end
One has arrived
All is beautiful
And there
Is such
Exquisite simplicity
Engulfing the
Totality of
Of all that is
One has arrived
Happiness is no
Longer sought
And Self is
Here.

—Seeking

The brilliance is vast
Beyond measure
The details
Dissipate
Into a silent
Bliss
And what
Is left
Is
Essence.

—Core

A soft peace sweeps over the beauty of Allness. Tranquility penetrates through, and one has arrived. Formlessness. Any resistance has been swept away by the serenity of consciousness. "It" is truly breathtaking. There is no longer a captivation around the fleetingness of duality. It arises, and then one sinks back into this formlessness. The senses have dissolved into this Allness. Emptiness, or one could say boundlessness. Where limitations are no longer present, for one is the Presence. Remarkable. Blessed it be, laughing at the splendor that emerges when one has remembered the presence of God. Brahman. God, in this moment.

—Here

When the unbelievable
Becomes believable
As the fallacious
Facts have been
Stripped from
The mind
And surrendered
To something
Of the highest
Glory
No-thing
Surrendered
To the merciful
Loving light
Of Presence.

—Reshaping the World

A gentle submission
Awakens the humility
Within the devoted
Spirit seeking
The One.

—Path

Welcome death
As a guest of
Boundlessness
Liberation
Is emanated from
The truth of
Existence
And death
Is no longer
Feared
But embraced
With a loving
Serenity
In stillness
All shall
Meet.

—Celebrate

May all paths
Lead to the
Discernment
Of truth
And all that is true
Glows an
Ineffable radiance
Of pure love
That knows
No bounds
And dances
Infinitely
As the sea
Of existence.

—Joyous

There is a certain fragility within conceptual thinking. For the mind seeks to validate, to prove, to discover, to create and so forth. It really goes on, and on, and on. Truly laughable. It does not want to stop. For if it stops, then what? And one might ask, stop for what? And then, thinking for what? And so forth. On, and on, and on, and on. Its destiny is based off one of illusion. Feeding itself for survival. The fear of death. For when thoughts cease, what happens? What gloriousness may arise from the empty mind that the mind is so fearful of. And every empty space that arises, thoughts eagerly fill. Must keep going. And so it goes like this, on and on and on. Think this. Think that. Know this. Know that. And the mind claims it knows everything. It has intellectualized every bit of information, experiences, and feelings. So, it knows. It has created a program to adhere to. But one must continue to feed the thoughts so the program can run, otherwise it will be at its demise. And this is truly it. It is not death that one fears, but "losing" one's mind. In losing one's mind, control is surrendered and the subjective is welcomed. And this is where love prevails, for love is not a state of the mind, but a state of being.

—Circles

The osprey flies through the expansive skies with fearlessness and tenacity. It pierces through the golden sun rays, as if it were the sun. All mighty and majestic. It is enveloped by the sun, as the sun. Becoming one with the sun. For it does not fear the light. It does not fear its deepest desires. It dives directly into Truth with unwavering strength and stillness. Its magnetism is revered. Its patience is honored. Its tenacity, inspiring. And it takes these gifts and dives deeply into the sifting waters at high speed. It goes into the depths of darkness with a knowingness that is beyond. For it is destined to catch its prey. And the osprey does not look to the sun, or to the turbulent dark waters with judgement. It embraces both elements exactly as they are. It merges with elements. Merges with All. For in its radical authenticity, it teaches that God resides within All. So, dive into the depths of darkness, for there will always be a light shining upon All.

—Merging

May joy blossom
With a gleeful
Grace
From the heart
When understanding
Is the foundation
Of every
Experience.

—Honor

In formlessness
Emerges the
Eternity of love
Returning to
Innocence
The essence
Of One
This is the
True state of
BEing.

—Silent

There is a gentle
Ambiance pulsating
Through Existence
God breathes
A breath of
Peace
And softness
Envelops all that is
Nurturing tones
Of brilliance
Sift through
Isness
And the miracles
Of Presence
Arrive in this
Moment
Infinitely on.

—Rhythm

There is nothing to do. So, rest the busy-ness. Rest the overthinkingness. Rest, beloved. For it can be frightening to surrender to the inevitable. That gentle calling to come home. To Self. The unknown. It whispers its song of serenity. Sweet loving serenity. Peace. Tranquility. Bliss. Ineffable. The Presence, is here. Now. Where miracles dance within the moment, this moment. And laughter prevails. And thinking subsides. Gently. Put it to rest. There is nothing to do. Only be. For the mind has created its to do list. And the heart emanates radical truth. Embrace being. Be.

—Radical

All is
An Emanation
Of God.

—Let God Be

With great joy, humility becomes the cornerstone of one's deepest devotion towards God. For in this path, every experience is welcomed with gratitude and patience. And what was seen as pain or conflict now is resolved so effortlessly with love and mercy. Everything is welcomed with open arms, and a soft smiling heart. The realm of duality dissolves in the presence of this humility, the tough edges bloom inexhaustibly as merely Presence. It is a joy to be open. To love without discernment, but an open heart aching to love all that it can. For this love knows of no bounds, and delights in mercy and understanding. It giggles with glee as it sinks itself as one with eternity.

—Gifts of Humility

In the timeless
Dimension of now
Lives an unbridled
Bliss ripening
In its becoming
A blooming
Magnificence
As it unfolds
Into a
Spacious
Presence.

—Flower

Gently sinking into the aloneness. The solitude that was once avoided at all costs. Surrendered distractions. Alone. Now embraced with a deep reverence. The whispers of God are met with stillness. And welcomed with delight. The quietness is a home of welcome. Peace and joy arise in the midst of this spaciousness. The absence of all that is untrue, leaves only the Presence. The Truth. Beauty and perfection flow through Presence. Existence is remarkable. Complete in its Completeness. Perfect in its unfolding of this very now. Beautiful in its totality. Hold the hand of God, an All will be revealed. The perfection that simply is. For All is All. And All is beautiful. All is Complete. All, is.

—Awe

Love has its sweet and tender way of smoothing over edges that were meant to simply "be." All that was in the closet, comes out of hiding in the presence of love. For in the presence of love, one sinks into unboundedness. All defenses, fears, and protection are emancipated. The illimitable presence of love is welcoming, as its very essence is of truth and purity. Seeing beyond, its love sees the beauty and perfection of all that is. For love dives straight into essence. And the essence of All that is, is Perfection.

—Soft

Kiss the bliss within
Watch as the
Miracle of
Transfiguration
Takes place.

—In

And suddenly, the persistent thinkingness comes to a halt. A dead end. All thoughts cease. And in this nowness arises a feeling of everythingness. An infallible connectedness to all that is. In full surrendering of the mind, one has become the All. Suchness. Thatness. Allness. A beautiful splendor of exquisite delight. Sigh. One is the sigh. Omniscience. The little self is engulfed by the Self. True Self has been revealed. The all wise. Truly impeccable. In this state of perfection, Existence is It. The illusionary shackles of the mind have dissolved and one is free to dance with God. Twirl in Presence. It is heavenly. And this heavenliness isn't up there, or over there. This heavenliness is right here. Alwaysness. Infinitely the light shines, for it is a beacon of truth. And Truth rests in the presence of God. In the presence of It. And one has become It.

—Remember

Swept away by the ecstasy
The immaculate beauty
Gleams effortlessly
And in this pureness
Innocence prevails
Igniting the child like
Wonder in all that is
And everything is
Perfect
All is Divine
And one can only
Smile at this simple
Revelation
For when one
Remembers the truth
Nothing is less
Than perfect.

—Heart Space

Love shows up everywhere. Within the blooming flowers. The gloom filled skies. The dolphins dancing in the ocean. The deep sigh of relief. The trees rooted into the earth. The child filled with laughter. The roaring city at night. The gleaming sun. The birthing of a newborn child. The field of daisies. The group of volunteers dedicated in selfless service. The loss of a parent. The fire crackling at midnight. The snow kissing the earth. The hug from a friend. The sound of music. The vibrant colors of life. The acceptance of a team. The joyous crowd at a football game. Sinking feet into the sand. The smell of salt water. Daydreaming. Crying. Healing. Dancing. Painting. Hiking. Love. Love. Love. Love. Love appears everywhere. Love is seen in everything. And felt beyond. For one has become it. Immersed so deeply in that of unconditional love, love simply expresses itself in all the ways. Love is omnipresent. Omnipotent. Love is All that is. May one have the courage to embody the love that is within. For love is calling All. And All is love.

—Come

And those noisy neighbors, those silly thoughts. Can sometimes be so beautiful. Thinking of the infinite. Thoughts beyond what is. And miracles arise when conceptual thought steps outside its comfort zone, standing on a precipice for innovation. In conjunction with faith, miracles are not expected but simply arise in the continuous moment. For the more loving the thought, the more power the thought has. And the more power the thought has, the more impactful the thought is. And the more impactful the thought is, the more transformative the thought can be to all in its vicinity. Thoughts, those funny thoughts can sometimes be noisy, but one simple thought could impact All that is. Remember this, and make every thought count. Be friends with neighbors, for these neighbors could be the next inventors, shifting All that is.

—Frequency

Dropping into awareness. The seat of Presence. In this silence, a deep peace breathes its breath of stillness. The veil has lifted. Truth is here. Serenity, now. That once fragile mind no longer persists. And the one is the One. The need for another is gone. For there is no other. One now basks as the eternal Presence of God. For One is the All. How beautiful. How lovely. Sinking into awareness. One becomes it. This blissful state is welcome to All. For God is always present. And Presence is always present. And when surrendering the mind, one can only be Presence. For all duality has dissolved, and alwaysness is here. In Being, one is the Presence. That all-encompassing love, joy, and peace. Truly. Deeply. Freely.

—Free to Be

Manifesting the unmanifest
The power
Behind consciousness
-Existence-
Is a phenomenon
Beyond comprehension
For it is
Ungraspable
And can only
Be experienced
In the present
Moment
-Now-
For this is
It
This is All
Consciousness
Is the all pervading
Presence enveloping
All with
Infinite love and
Bliss
It is
Ever present.

—Nowness

In the realm of consciousness, all humanness is perfect exactly the way it is in this moment. Absolutely beautiful. All those things deemed as an "error" or "mistake" simply arise out of limitation from the mind. For all is exactly how all can be within each given moment, otherwise it would be different. So, when anger arises out of being lied to, this is only a limitation. And instead of working against limitation, working with limitation will help one move through limitation, into a state of infinite grace. A state of peace. Presence. This is God.

—Dance with the Unlimited

Waking from a restless slumber. Fell back asleep. A deep, deep sleep. Fell into an illusion. Fell into a deep, deep illusion. Quite unreal. What is even real. Looking around a form filled illusion. Take a few steps back. Slowly. Wake up. Waking up. Abruptly. Surprisingly. Waking up from the deep, deep sleep. Waking up from the deep, deep illusion. Waking up from the programming. Returning to the truth. Returning to innocence. Returning to consciousness, existence, bliss. Returning to eternity. Returning to this moment. Can't fall back asleep. No longer can fall asleep. Too awake. Too aware. Noticing. Recognizing. What is truth, and what is absent of truth. For once one has tasted what it is to be awake, the illusion will no longer have the same pull. The shackles have been released. One is free. One has always been free. God is present, always. Breathe deep. Breathe deep beloved. Wake up and simply be.

—Deep Deep

May the love of Existence
Radiate into All
For the beauty of
Existence is
An eternal mastery
Of glimmering
Goodness
-Sigh-
What a beloved
Precious
Gift to witness
It is in this moment
One shall
Recognize this
Divine gift.

—Now

It all becomes a little softer. A little more subtle. The softness sweeps over. And such softness smooths every rugged edge. Not by force, for this softness is so delicate and loving in its nature the rugged edge would not even notice the effect of softness. Meanwhile, the rugged edges are disintegrating, smoothing over. Ever so lightly. Ever so peacefully. The divine love emanates into the core of the rugged edges, unraveling the tight grip. The grip loosens as it is enveloped with the softness of Divinity. Grace sifts through and around, holding the rugged edges in a warm embrace. The rugged edges crumble inside, jagged edges falling to the side. And what is left is a smoothed over cliff. A steady stillness. A once rough-edged cliff, stands firmly with its softened view. For it has been washed over by the power of love. And the power of love heals. It softens. It loves. Boundlessly. Unconditionally.

—JWM

The pot of gold
Shines its brilliant
Beloved light
The pot of gold
Is a spark
Of love
Blossoming
From the divine
The pot of gold
Is not somewhere
To be found
Out there
The pot of gold
Is to be found
Within
Breathe in
Right here

—Gifts

Returning to the soft center
Where kindness blooms
From a boundless
Nothingness
And an unshakeable emptiness
Rises in peace.

—Home Bound

One must be here. For there is nothing to do. And no place to go. One must simply be here. In the now. Be. In this impeccable moment. This is the juice. This is bliss. This is the essence of being. Where distractions are no longer distractions, and all simply is. And Self is Existence. Not the little self; me, my, myself, I. No not this self. Self as totality. Self as all that Is. God. Brahman. Self as revealed as God manifest. Illusions are stripped away in Presence. Self as Presence. Self as Allness. Consciousness. The unraveling of an illusionary reality, enveloped by Self. God manifest. The boundless peace awaiting, here. For there is nothing to do. And no place to go. One must simply be here, now. In this moment. And be in the bliss of Self. Omnipotence.

—Selfless

Waves of light shine through, bursting through crackling shadows. The fears are swallowed by a sea of Grace. And enveloped by the infinite Presence. Bringing love and light to the depth. To the hollow. To the hidden. Shining boundless light into the dark. Waves of peace arise as the shadow unfurls. All clinging is released. Shame is melted as Love cascades over. The shadow is no longer separated but immersed in this divine light. It blends with the All, for All is inclusive. The light penetrates the core of the shadow, bringing forth its brilliance. Its beloved gifts. Showering in the presence of infinite light. The shadow reveals its inherent light. And All bursts into flames of light. Face the shadow, and be immersed in the Divine. All is All. All is Divine.

—Unity

Dance joyously in the uninhibited state of being. Being, embracing the All. Allowing the Divine to flow through effortlessly. For All is an embodiment of God. Feel the splendor in letting go. Being enveloped by a remarkable Presence. It takes over, and the mind goes blank. Without thought, joyously in freedom. Spreading wings, taking flight. Shifting to new levels of awareness. Breaking through paradigms. Immersed in the inclusivity of the Allness. Flying, floating, expanding. Evolving, elevating. Dancing joyously in the expansive state of beingness. Where all resistance is fallen to the side, and faith is fully embraced. Beautiful beloveds, sink into the faith. Trust in All, for All is the All. Trust this letting go. Be, as Totality.

—Elevate

Even when fear is far
Or near
So tell the fear
To come a little closer
And wrap it in a cocoon
Of Presence
Watching it dissolve
Into a puddle
Of Divinity.

—Near

And sometimes love seems far off
In the distance
-Can't seem to wrap these brittle fingers around it
to enclose it-
To hold it close
Holding on for dear life
Keeping it close
But in the holding
The infinite love that is surrounding
Seems to be missed
Still holding and keeping it near
The one pointed focus
On entrapping this love
Is calculated by the minds
Need to control
But it is in complete submission
That one is able to
Really allow
And sink into this
Divine love
That is permeating
All of existence
For when righteousness is
Surrendered
And one bows down
To the divinity
Within all

Infinite love
Comes streaming in
Through the floodgates
And one arrives
At the hearts
Deepest longing
To return
To the innocence
And purity
That is breathing
Within
This innocence
Is at the heart
Of All that is
Blossoming from
Existence, Consciousness, Bliss.

—Focus

There is a fragility of the mind that softens as the details fritter away. As the opinions and judgements are lightly confronted by experience, one is able to deeply let go of all the tightly held projections and perceptions that have long been stored as a protection mechanism of the mind. For the mind thinks it needs protection, to keep its thinkingness safe. For what happens when thinkingness dwindles away and one is left with the softest silence. The mind loves to be busy, to be filled with the pleasures of tomorrow and the regrets of yesterday. Anything to occupy and keep it filled, to keep it going. It feels safe in its thinkingness. It is satisfied with all of life's distractions. It seeks distraction, for this is the food of the mind. Without distractions, how would the mind survive. What happens when the mind is stripped of food and left to surrender in silence. To simply be enveloped by the quietness of this exquisite universe. The mind unfurls in the Presence, the all-pervading peace. It begins to unravel, and in this unraveling it begins to experience the unfettered joy that is Existence. And the mind begins to release resistance of this all-encompassing love, softening it a bit more. And it starts to become a little more quiet, and less distractions are sought. And then the distractions are no longer distractions. And the mind fades into the All, becoming the All, as the All. And there are no more distractions, for One is the All. There is the One Mind.

—Distractions

Whispers of the divine sprinkle through, and Existence continues to light up from the twinkle of the Divine breathing through All that is. The whispers get louder and louder, and the world becomes brighter and brighter. Expanding into higher consciousness. Shifting into an unbounded state of unconditional love, joy and peace. Shaking off the debris of yesterday and embracing the love of now. All fears are washed away by this Divine Presence. The world is brighter than bright, it is on fire. And it is here, the world says yes to right now. The world says yes to the Eternal Now. Everything is lit up, all has a glistening glow that is emanating a graceful joy. There is an unshakeable silence washing over All that is, leaving a touch of kindness. And this kindness ripples into the ethers. Consciousness is continuously shifting, and as it shifts All that is expands into an effervescent glowing boundless ray of light. The world is on fire, it is the sunshine of the universe. This is the brightest show in the galaxy, take a moment to watch this brilliant beauty gleam like it never has before.

—Observer

Speak the truth
Emanating from the heart
Let it flow
Like a river
Of God's love
And allow it to
Wash away
Every untruth
Layered in layers
Ready to be
Awakened to the blissful
Loving peace
Streaming through
All that is
Speak the truth
And watch as
It gently
Caresses all pain
Into a gentle
Submission
Allowing the light to flow
Through it
And become
One with
All that is
Unfolding as
Perfect
Existence.

—Speak

It is ok to stop right there
Stop and embrace
The quietude of this
Very moment
It is ok to sink further
Into this Eternal Now
Letting go into
The vastness
-Emptiness-
And it is ok to float
Float like a river
Of love
Right here
Flowing as a steady
Stream of perfection
It is ok to deepen
The surrender
Falling further into
All that is
As the All
For God is permeating
All of existence
Living and breathing
Through All that is
And it only takes
This moment
Right here

For one to truly
Witness God
This Presence
This Divinity
That is not out there
But inherent
In All
For Divinity
Dances within.

—OK

The seeds within are ripening to the magnificent beauty that is, has been, and always will be, for this is the truth. Unwavering, and unbounded. A soft summer breeze cools the feet, planted firmly into the finite, swaying with the luscious green trees, drifting, floating, flowing, becoming and unbecoming as the infinite, the All. The seeds are ripening, becoming and unbecoming as Infinity.

—Willow

Nothing but a smile
On the face
Laughter spilling
From the heart
And love blooming
From the pocket
What a joyous
Liberation
To be.

—Just Be

Enchanted by the miracles
Of this everlasting moment
Breathing in the beauty
Dancing ubiquitously
Within the All
Smiling
For all suchness
Is of radiant
Perfection
Simply divine
The exquisiteness
Of the All
Gleams like that
Of the sun as the light
Continues to expand
The miracles unfolding
Of this moment
Become a constant
And the inherent
Bliss arises for
All to bask
In Divinity.

—Blushing

Sweet serendipitous
Dance of this blissful earth
Shimmering in gladness
And kindness
Sprinkled through the breath
Of all that is
Joy frolicking
Rainbows enveloping
The atmosphere
The whisperings
Of I
Becoming more
Clear.

—Transfiguration

Taking a step back. Allowing the big picture to step into its fullness. Stepping out of front row seating, to have a more expansive view, for one can get lost in the realm of tunnel vision and such narrowness. Breathe. Expand further. Take a step back, allowing things to be exactly as they are. Not as the narrow mind imagines it all to be. And the further one steps back, one is able to soak in the grandness of life and all its beautiful glory. One is able to see the perfection of what is, instead of its own perceived state of perfection. And when narrowness dissolves into the infinitude, the magnificent perfection that is becomes a blissful breathtaking view. A heaven on earth, and one no longer need to escape it. For it is right here, beloved.

—Picture

The earth glows
As the hearts
Radiate an immanent
Nurturing light
Of ease and
Calmness
A silence
Takes over
-Hush-
All is still
The moment
This moment
Is here
A unified
Awakening
Bursts through
Ever so softly
-Cracked open-
Suddenly
It is revealed
The truth of all
Truths
God is here.

—The Finale

Frolicking
Peacefully
In service
To the God
In all of Thee.

—Simplicity

There are many avenues to God, for God is omnipresent, omnipotent. There is no specific way or path in devotion to God. God hears, and is always present. Therefore, there are no mistakes, no rights or wrongs, no proofs, only that one is truly devoted to God. And in this, one continues to surrender, ripening, when at last the light is revealed to itself. Enlightenment is available to all. God is Omnipresent, wherever one is, God is there too.

—Free Will

Fleeting flickering light
Bright
Bright
Bright
Light of light
Always
There
Simply be
An unbridled
Heart
Is the
Eternal
Key.

—Surrendering

Peace rises
Up the spine
Unwavering in
Its stillness
Mercifully kissing
The edges
Of the magnetic field
Of bountiful
Ecstasy.

—Omnipotent

A field of
Boundless peace
Breathes through
The rhythm
Of the pulsating
Heart of
Isness.

—Knowingness

Vibrations sifting
Through the
Heart of the
Divine
Singing eloquent
Tones
Of spiritual
Brilliance
A madness
That is
So delightful
One is
Enveloped in
Rapture.

—Shine

Sweet surrender in serenity, a tranquil union of divinity, gleeful universe. Consciousness filled with love, joy, peace. Breathing in the breath of shimmering gold light, soaking in the sweetness, the magic, the ineffable, the perfection that simply is.

—All

A quiet inner bliss
Rises through
Beingness
Quivering in ecstasy
It is the truth
The stillness
The peace
Of Presence
Where all distractions
Dissolve
And one is
Aware
And Complete.

—Truth

Ride the wave
All the way through
And through
This through-ness
One enters into
A boundless existence
An eternal dance
With limitlessness
Joyousness
Peace.

—Limitless

Take a step back
Take another step back
Take another
And another
Take as many steps back
As needed
Or wanted
For one is
Not "in" it
One is
Simply
All.

—Equanimity

Ubiquitous beauty. Beautiful beauty. Perfect. Palpable. And the beauty never runs out or disappears. For it is always here, always Present. Even in moments of despair. Adversity. In inexpressible grief. Apathy. For beauty encapsulates the eternal moment. It is the mind that is unable to grasp this. In conceptual thinking, barriers arise as the mind forms opinions and judgements of how Existence ought to be. When these thoughts are released, and the worn out belief systems are given way, the beauty of all that is reveals itself. Beauty is always present. In the realm of nonlinear, one does not need to make sense of anything for all is perfect. Perfection is embraced in its totality. Its ism-ness. For the mind can only perceive a glimpse into what truly is. See, anything that is of truth does not need to be held onto. So, one must ask the question, what must be held so tightly? What for? What is so important that one must bypass the eternal beauty gleaming in this exact moment. Pause in this, and surrender to the beauty of All that is.

—Perfect Existence

May the warmth of grace wrap the delicate earth in a golden sheath of unconditional love. A cozy embrace, where pain has its space to unfurl alongside the river of beauty and miracles. A sea of glistening waters, like tear drops, soften the edges with infinite compassion. A boundlessness so vast, only God knows. Drops of glitter sprinkle into the vastness, lightening up all that is to be revealed. Revelation. The softest surrender, dropping into the beauty of it all. All fallacy is washed away by the ubiquitous joy sprinkling gladness throughout. Rest in the space of splendor. Radically authentic. Free. Spacious. And so it is.

—Bless it Be

A shift in consciousness
Recalibrates
That totality
Of all that is
For every thought
Decision
Behavior
Intention
Has been recorded
In the unmanifest
The eternal
Not subject to
Division or separation
A sublime
Inclusivity
That is only
Embraced
As perfection.

—One

Sometimes there is a joy so merry, one can only laugh. Sometimes there is a happiness so loud, tears of joy sprinkle upon the earth. Sometimes there is a lightheartedness so vibrant, all remember innocence. Sometimes it is so merry, bubbles of cheer spring forth from every heart. And sometimes there is a bliss so heavenly, Self is revealed. Completely.

—Divinely

The Presence
Is engulfing
In its formlessness
Transmitting
The truth
Of God
Within
This joyous
Moment.

—Gracious

There were no longer tears shed from sorrow, or the ineffable grief. But tears of infallible joy and bliss. A joy so open, laughter began to beam through the heart center like that of the sun. Expansively, lovingly, giving light to all. All inclusive. Deep reverence shined through to All. How glorious, to shine a light upon all that is without any discernment, only pure love. To give, without any expectations. To love with no conditions. This innocence is the essence of Existence. And All have free will to tap into the Divinity resting deep within. For when this divinity is embraced within, only perfection can be seen without. Absolute perfection. Beauty. And tranquility becomes the continuous emanation of All that is. Here, and now.

—Tranquility

God buried a flame
So deep
Within All
That it
Is inevitable
For it not to
Be ignited
May any confusion
Or doubt
Lead one to
The depths
Of this
Burning flame
Of infinite love
Guiding all
To the immanent
Truth.

—Home

A benevolent existence. One of vastness beyond vast. Empty of restrictions. Absolute in its entirety. Formlessness so eloquent in its boundlessness, it seeks nothing and is all that is. A beautiful treasure. One that cannot be thought of, or felt. For one is already "it." The radiance of the Allness twinkles in innocence. Pure. Divine. Existence is it. And wherever one goes, existence is "there" too.

—Vastness

And for a split second, the presence of God became all consuming. All such thinkingness and doingness stopped. It just stopped. Completely. Or did it stop? Perhaps, there was no one to think, or to do. Where did "I" go. Gone. Blissfully, the emergence of this Presence was all there was. Is. This moment, infinite. Without edges. As if it were the All. All such seeking, dissolved. For this Presence was simply it. It is simply it. A bliss so palpable, tears of joy surface. And what is left is no longer self, but the true Self. The I Am. Brahman. God. Existence. A sigh of ecstasy for this return home. All is the All. And so it is.

—I AM

A continuous flow
Of the now
Allows the heart
To dance like a butterfly
In a limitless
Presence
And dive back
Into the innocence
Of simply
Being.

—Purity

The silky fragrance of
Lavender weaves its
Softness through
Dancing flowers
And unwavering trees
Laughing clouds
And an effervescent
Sun sparkling its
Light upon All
That is
With reverence
For it is truly
A noble path
To embody
That of
Divine love.

—Unconditional

Like that of a tree
When in a state
Of Being
-Total Surrender-
Every response
Is spontaneous
And with unwavering
Peace
And Serenity
For there is no
Push or pull
All is absolutely
Perfect
Beyond perfection
So anything
That arises
Is welcomed and accepted
With a loving
Grace
And seen as
Complete.

—Perfection

From consciousness arises the potentiality of all that is. It is a field of unshakeable Presence. For it is the Presence. What is known as God. Or Brahman. Or Oneness. Formlessness. Pure consciousness is everything. Unmanifest, manifest. There is no such "thing" in it, even though it is full of everything. And consciousness can be likened to awareness. So, when one arrives in the state of awareness, one is embodying this Presence. One is It. When attachments are abdicated, one by one, this Presence expands until all attachments are relinquished. And just like that, there is no longer any reaching or wondering with the mind. For the mind has dissolved into this pure state of awareness. And All is the All. May all rest in the peaceful Presence, that is All.

—Oneness

All is complete
In itself
All is within
The All
And perfection
Completeness
Bliss
And beauty
Emanate
As the All.

—Divine

Out of awareness arises the questioning and surrendering. Dismantling deeply engrained beliefs. Those are not to keep. Let go. And wishing to hold ever so tightly to this beloved idea, opinion, judgement, concept. It is followed with a simple yet profound, what for? Watch the attachment dissolve right then and there. As it is has been given permission to breathe. To be set free. If one must hold tightly, and that is ok too. For all is simply perfect as it is. Out of awareness arises a power that is beyond man's creation. It is the power of Spirit, God, Presence. And this is the power that moves not only mountains, but humanity, consciousness itself. All is consciousness, and it is a collective effort in the continuous shifting of this eternal perfection of now. And with awareness, one has the choice to participate. To embrace the totality of all that is, revealing its remarkable purity, innocence, and perfection. When All is revealed to All, what is truly ineffable has arrived. And this is it. This is It.

—All in All

Existence
Is an endless
Wave of consciousness
Marveling in
A stream
Of infinite
Bliss
Shining
Its perfection
Joyously
As the merciful
All.

—Ocean

Respect does not arise out of one's perfected state of being. Respect is a surrender to the authentic beauty that encapsulates life. This respect stems from humility, from the love of God. From the compassion and understanding of unconditional love. From Presence. This respect is for All that is, as it is. For All is perfect as it is in this moment. All is doing its best. And this is in truth, otherwise All would do different. There is much respect and appreciation for All that is. Without conditions or ideas of what deserves to have respect. No, in this sense respect has been surrendered to God. For in the Presence of God, there are no conditions or filters. And All is respected. All is perfect. All is beautiful. Surrender beloveds, for the respect that is All. For it is a blessed gift. A divine gift.

—Bow

In this completeness
There is a humbling release
Of all knowingness
And reverence for
All that Is
This completeness
Is so inclusive
That one
Is immersed
In its totality
No longer vulnerable
But powerful
In its Completeness
-Deep breath-
How beautiful
To embrace
The divinity within
So as to
-Be-
Divinity in all
That is.

—Wholeness

A beam of lightening strikes, and the mind twirls out of its cocoon. Shaking off the debris. Shaking off the tightly held beliefs. Unraveling into creation, for this is evolution. And it is true, these are one in the same. It is a continuous blossoming, unfolding, unraveling, unmanifest to manifest in a sea of consciousness. For it cannot destroy itself, it can only shift its frequency. And this is Divinity itself. A continuous creation of delight, that happens to be one miraculous moment deemed as evolution. Such magnificence cannot be labeled, for its magnificence is formless. It is only brought to form to understand, reason, grasp with the reaching mind. But no mind is truly necessary to dive into the truth, just a big leap of faith and total surrender. The dance of creation, evolution is an exquisite one. Creation manifests through the unmanifest, formlessness. What a beautiful phenomenon. As evolution continues, creation is along for the ride. There is no separation within divinity, for all is derived from formlessness. A boundless ocean of Existence.

—Evolution as Creation

Look at the beautiful world
The marvelous and divine
Beauty shimmering within
Look at the beauty within
Sit with it
Be with it
Breathe it in
Just for a moment
For the beauty within shines without
It beams out into
All that is
Cascading with infinite
Serenity and peace
And so it
Is called
Creation
-What is being created-
Beloved
Look deep enough
It is beauty
That one will
See.

—Creativity

A joyous laughter. A laughter so contagious, the whole world is twirling in infinite glee. This is the innocence, the essence of being. Where joy is spilling out of the chest, and love is sifting fervently through All. This love heals. This love soothes. This love nurtures. Nestling gently into those once dark spaces. Now shining brighter than bright. The laughter is so loud, the heart begins brimming with infallible peace. Pure joy. Emanating from within. This is the essence of All that is.

—Glee

The paradox of life is truly laughable. At the core of Existence, the very essence of it lay a subtle humor. For such a happening. And one must simply laugh. Because it is quite humorous. It does not need to be taken so seriously. How funny. Taking something so seriously that at its very essence, is laughable. Innocent. Pure. And this makes it all the more laughable. And this is the way. Laughing the way through. Shaking off all resistance with an infallible joy and lightness. For when one has arrived here, the paradox is seen in all its beauty and perfection. Its lightness. Laugh it up, beloved.

—Laugh Away

A joyous glee
Simmering beneath
The surface
One may almost
Rupture
As the laughter
Spills out of the
Chest and burns
Through all fear
And grief
The ashes
Are kissed with
Humility
And a touch
Of grace
This shining moment
Of boundless perfection
Reveals that All
Are enveloped
In the love
Of this
Infinite Presence.

—Bodhi

And sometimes it is so easy
To get swept away
By all the things
All the little things
Darn things
Distractions are plentiful
Yet surrounded by something
That is subtle yet
Magnificent
-God-
So get swept away
In the little things
All the things
Fully be immersed
In these things
For God
Is always present
And within a blink
Of an eye
Those things will
No longer matter
And the focus will
Shift into the essence
Of Existence
-God-
And one will laugh
At such things
Surrendering
To eternity.

—Little Things

There is infinite power swirling through as Existence. Endless possibilities, encapsulated by boundlessness. Infinitude. Magnificence. Brilliance. Divinity. Existence is the blossoming of consciousness. An ever expansiveness. Thriving as an unbounded masterpiece. It thrives in its Completeness. It delights in uncertainty. Surrounding all paradoxes with humor. All that ordinary and suchness is embraced with vastness. Within consciousness blooms the extraordinary. Delving into limitlessness, absent of limitation. For beauty ripples through the ethers and beyond. Beyond, and right here. Is the silent beauty gleefully smiling through the All. This suchness, beyond words. This suchness, beyond imagination. This suchness emanating from the Divine. Through the All.

—Exquisite

Silky smooth softness
Delicate dancing divine
Blissfully brilliant beauty
Shining shimmering starlight
Glistening gleefully gladness
Humble honest honoring
Transcendent twirling twinkle
Colorful caring compassion
Intuitive immanent intimacy
Enlightened emanating exquisiteness
Fruitful faithful frolicking
Nurturing noble nature
Miraculous marvelous moment
Visionary vivacious view
Open omniscient oneness
Benevolent benign beginning
Jovial joyous jolly
Wonderful wisdom written
Peacefully present path
-Be here now-
Remarkability rest renew
And be still
Be blessed
Simply be.

—Twirl

Omnipotence rests in stillness. In the resting heart open to the divinity within this very moment. It gleefully immerses into the vastness of the Allness. The boundlessness emanating as Existence. Omnipresence arises, the moment one surrenders to the Presence within. God. Brahman. Consciousness. And as one surrenders one is enveloped by the infiniteness of All that is. Becoming fully aware that One is the All. And All is One. The realm of consciousness is without limitations, for all is inclusive. Nothing is left out, alone. And everything is the All. For all is derived from this suchness. This Allness, that is All. Consciousness is the inclusiveness of all that is, rippling its mighty loving compassion into the ethers. There is infinite peace awaiting All.

—Openness

The moment where
All have awakened
To the truth
Beating within
It is here
May all rejoice
As Divinity.

—Homecoming

Sprinkling unfettered joy generously, as a being of love and light. Sprinkling droplets of peace, for this is the essence that is All. Sprinkling trickles of ecstasy, for All is lit up. Sprinkling speckles of love, for Existence is of the infinitude dancing in a belly of unconditional love. Sprinkling boundless compassion, cracking open the heart of All for the love of God to sift through and melt away the jagged edges. Sprinkling infinite gratitude, for the beauty and perfection that is All. Sitting with the ineffable, sprinkling tears of infallible joy.

—Sprinkle Sprinkle

As one sinks further into
This boundless existence
Wings of faith and reverence
Blossom with a gentle glow
And One is able to experience
The Presence
Diving further into the unknown
Breaking through paradigms
Shifting consciousness
Allowing the ineffable
To shine through
In its highest glory
All expands
And in this expansion
Allows infinite waves
Of peace to cascade
Through all that is
As consciousness shifts
All is deeply moved
By this penetrating
Stillness enveloped
By peace
And like wildfire
It spreads
Miraculously
Lovingly
Joyously.

—Benevolence

Serenity kisses the twinkling
Untethered skies filled
With remarkable brilliance
Tranquility sprinkles
Into All that is
A permeating softness
Envelops existence
Dissolving all
Righteousness
The mind becoming still
The truth is near
Illusion washing away
Fear relinquished
Love embracing
Grace falling from
The shimmering sky
The mind has let go
Becoming as the All
In a boundless state
Floating in
Infinite bliss
The mind no longer
Reaches
For the truth
Is right here.

—Ever Present

Sit back
And get a little
Back scratching
Feel the warm
Fuzzies of God
Dripping through
The essence
Of Being
Blissful beauty
Dancing like
A beaming ray
Of sunshine
Benevolence oozing
Off each ray
Pearls of wisdom
Twinkling as a
A light of infinitude
The light within
So vibrant
So pure
Rippling through
The edges of
Existence
Shattering boundaries
And blending
All that is
As one magnificent

Creation
Of shimmering light
That gleams
Simply as a Presence
-Be-
For a moment
And bask in the
Unbounded light
Shining within
A beautiful star
Exploding into bits
Of bliss
Kissing all that
Is.

—Listen to God Within
(Collaboration with Gabriella)

Sitting here, in a state of ecstatic peace. A peace beyond what the mind imagines, for the mind has been cradled like a baby falling fast asleep into a blissful state of complete awareness. Fully aware of the now. And in the presence of Now, unfettered joy sifts its way through. Boundlessly. Ecstatically. Generously. The mind, at deep peace as it lays down all of its holding. Surrendering its tight grip, submitting to the flow of All that Is. Gently letting go, and falling into the steady river of consciousness. Flowing, so softly and naturally. Angelically. All simply flows. For consciousness is simply a beautiful flow of creation, from unmanifest to manifest. Flowing. It is Divine. All is Divine. All is Pure. All is Love. All flows, as a steady stream of divine perfection. For there is more to it than what any mind could ever perceive. Cradling the mind like a baby, and watch as it releases into the beautiful flow becoming and unbecoming. Blending into the All as the All. Becoming fully aware, the mind goes silent and peace streams through the floodgates. Unbounded peace.

—Fluidity

The path of peace is a gentle awakening to the perfection breathing within. A soft letting go of yesterday, and a warm release of tomorrow. A divine sinking into the flow of the Eternal Now. The Presence gleams, basking in its ordinariness, submitting to the beauty that simply is. The path of peace follows humility as a compass and with each moment one surrenders a little bit more. Bliss blossoms with the tender submission, and graces washes over with its angelic wings. All holding melts into the ecstatic Now, and one is in full submission. Complete. One. As the All.

—Submit

It is all falling apart and coming together. Contracting and expanding. Existence is shifting as consciousness shifts in this dance. This lovely perfect dance. Joy and grief, as one. Fear and love, as one. All as one. One is All. The world of opposites seems to disintegrate into the field of love, All that is. And those once opposites become another. As another. Breathing in and out of consciousness. For all is derived from this very source. And this very source is divine, exquisite, perfect in nature. And all that emanates and manifests from this source is simply perfect. Pure. Innocent. The ripples of fear, grief, and anger sink into the boundless Existence. Enveloped by this all loving Presence. And there is an ethereal quality to all that is. A delicate lightness. Like floating through infinitude. As the infinitude. Do not worry beloveds, All is being guided back toward the inherent light in this timeless dance. There is no rush, for the light is always here, Now. Shining its impeccable light as a selfless ray of beaming joy.

—Walking Home

Silky soft pulsations
Of the Divine
Dance like fluttering butterflies
Sprinkling pockets of glee
Right here and now
The perfection of
This moment
Shines like a beacon
Of light
Radiating the love
Of God
It is a delight
To be alive
It is a miracle
For such opportunity
To arise in this
Eternal Now
And as consciousness
Continues to
Evolve
Shifting and pulsating
The light beams
Brighter and brighter
The love expands
Further and further
And All deepen
Into the surrender

To Self
And this marvelous
Celebration
Brings deep reverence
Sprinkled with
Humility and a bounce
Of joy
Welcome home
Beautiful
Beloveds.

—Perfection of Divinity

Tick tock tick tock
Time is fleeting away
Tick tock tick tock
The truth is here
Tick tock tick tock
There is no time
On God's watch
Tick tock tick tock
The mind is dissolving
Into the All
Tick tock tick tock
Inhaling a deep
Breath of relaxation
Exhaling the passing
Of such time
In this all-pervading
Nowness
The whispers of
Divinity become heard
And the once deaf
Soak in the truth
And all marvel
In the revelation
Of this illusionary
Perception projected
From mind
Gently laying it all down

In complete surrender
All is enveloped
By the totality of
Existence
Its exquisite perfection
And infinite beauty
Shine forth
The All
As the All
Dance like a blissful
Bursting star
Of boundless
Perfection.

—Timelessness

All that reaching, and all that gathering and collecting comes to a slow halt. For consciousness is a steady stream of Allness, far beyond the tangible. And the linear is a beautiful safe place to be, perceived by the mind. Stay within this box, for everything outside of such box is not real. When truly everything that is in such box is unreal, and all that is beyond it is ineffable. And the mind is unable to comprehend the ineffable. Here arises the opportunity to break through the beloved mind, into the nonlinear dimension and dance in the realm of subjectivity. Where ambiguity and abstraction are embraced and the tangibles fade away like shooting stars. Chaos blends with perfection, and all such madness is Divine. The mind is a precious gift, a tool and such tool can be broken in. The mind likes its little box, sticking with the known. The concrete, the facts, the details. As the mind is tended to like a garden, the details fleet away, and the permanent becomes not so permanent. Things are not so concrete, and there are no such things. And everything becomes one subjective experience that is truly Divine. Remarkable. Breathtaking. The mind is a precious gift to be tended to with utmost appreciation and humility, for the seeds of revelation arise from here, the One Mind, Brahman, Existence.

—Tending the Garden

Fear brittles the bones, love softens
The fear into puddles of
Infallible joy
With great surrender
Becoming one another
As the other
As One.

—Allness

There's something a little
Funny about it all
Instead one shall
Retreat within
And continue to simmer
In this unspeakable bliss
For there are no words
To encapsulate such
The Ineffable.

—Speechless

A lightful life
One of grace
And divine
The beauty
So glorious
Everything
Effortlessly
Shines.

—Sparkle

Angelic teardrops drizzle
From the fuzzy blue sky
Shimmering waves of
Gold radiate through
Cotton candy clouds
Of bliss
The sun beaming its
Effervescent light
On all that is
And everything
Simply
Goes on being
Dancing among
The infinite wave
Of beauty
This is the perfection
Inherent
In All.

—Divine Being

Breathing in the beautiful moment, stillness sprinkles its quiet ecstasy throughout. Deeper and deeper into the breath, glistening white light begins to illuminate the spacious space of peace. Breathing in, arises boundlessness, one becomes the breath. One surrenders everything to God, breathing as the breath. Breathing the breath of God. Surrendering. Laying it down. Gently. Softly. Lovingly. Blissfully. Enveloped by the benevolence of all that is, tears of joy begin to dribble into, as the boundlessness. One is no longer breathing. One is all of it. Peace. Bliss. Ineffability springs forth. Thoughts are no longer present. There are no words that can encapsulate the brilliance of all that is. Self is revealed. Self is complete. Is, is.

—Ineffable

PERSPECTIVE FROM SELF

What a beautiful, exquisite emanation of God. A joyous beloved. How beautiful. There she is, dancing in such innocence and joy. A heart filled with unconditional love, a yearning to return home to a state of peace, joy and bliss. This is going to be such a beautiful journey. How glorious! She is already ready to dive deep, lovely how willing she is. To embrace the adversities of life with such openness. To welcome everything with such innocence. The struggle is beautiful. She is so beautiful, so divine.

One day she will see outside that number, and all those distractions just how lovely she is. One day this pain will no longer blind her from the immanent beauty that is life. That is unfurling inside her heart. And seeing just how lovely All is. And just how this loveliness emanates from All. It is beautiful for her to experience these things, for experience is such a beautiful teacher. And this pain is expanding so much compassion. So much perspective. She will use this pain, this pain may feel overwhelming at times but this pain will soon be her medicine. She is strong and wise. And one day she will see this. This pain has gotten so loud, but she is aware. She is fully aware and now she is listening to the pain. She is surrendering. She is letting go. Following the pain. Beautiful, she is leaning into the pain. She is holding it with tender compassion. She is being gentle and kind. She is learning to heal. That innocent joy is returning. And this joy is being sprinkled generously into her path, into all that is. She is embracing the gift of healing joyously. How beautiful and divine. She goes deeper and deeper into the healing. Finding more gifts and treasures. Finding love for herself. Embracing this love for herself. And sharing this love for humanity. Learning to love the humanity in humanity. Learning to accept the humanity in humanity. Finding the gifts and goodness in humanity. Seeing the perfection in all that is. Seeing the beauty in all that is. For the beauty she has found within is permeating Existence. The love she has embraced within, is extending into the All. The beauty within, ineffable. The love within, ineffable. The peace within, ineffable. And this beauty is seen in the All. This love is in the All. The peace is pervading all of existence. She continues to surrender to the infinitude. To the beauty that is life. The beauty that lives within. In a continuous state of surrender, she lives in state of gratitude surrounded by endless miracles. Her life has become a continuous miracle. One of synchronicity, and boundless joy and peace. She embraces All with love, and is inspired by a continuous state of humility. She embraces humility with such joy and gratitude. She is humbled, and in a state of unbounded bliss. Her life has become ineffable. There are no words that truly encapsulate this state. She has returned, home to the Essence of being. Existence, consciousness, bliss. The return to Self. Self as Existence. Brahman.

METTA PRAYER

May you be well. May you be happy. May you be free. May you be safe. May you be healthy. May you be filled with loving kindness. May you bask in the bliss breathing within. May you shine light, like that of the sun. May you smile simply because. May you laugh at the little things. May you nurture yourself always. May you continue to grow and expand. May you know you are Divine. May you feel your Perfection. May you see the beauty inherent in All. And may you be at peace and ease, beautiful Beloved.

OM MANI PADME HUM
(SANSKRIT MANTRA)

ABOUT CAITLIN LEIGH

This is Caitlin's fifth book of poetry that has been inspired by David R. Hawkins who was dedicated to studying consciousness. She has a Master's in Transpersonal Psychology with an emphasis in Ecopsychology and Life Coaching, along with several certifications in energy healing. Caitlin discovered that her resistance toward adversity was creating an internal cycle of suffering for over a decade; eating disorders, addictions, codependency, and mental health disorders. In the process, she discovered many healing modalities that helped alleviate some of the suffering, but not all. It was until she started reading about consciousness and the mind, that her attachment to this suffering began to lift. Caitlin was desperate not so much as to escape suffering, but to find the truth. With great devotion to God, and surrendering of the mind, Caitlin began to realize that all suffering is created by the mind. She immersed her heart into the readings of consciousness, along with Graced healings created by Diane Pfister and Energy Healing, and realized that there are no limits, and the limits that we bump into arise from conceptual thinking. From this realization, Caitlin has dedicated her life to releasing her attachment to thought forms and control, so as to embrace the peace of this very moment. This book has been assimilated from all of her readings and healings, and persistent dedication in embracing God, Presence, Existence, Bliss. May the truth be revealed in All, as All. Blessings!

SUPPORT

If you are interested in purchasing more of Caitlin's work, you may find them here:

- https://fluegge4.wixsite.com/caitlinleigh777
- https://www.etsy.com/shop/WordsofBodhi
- https://linktr.ee/caitlinleigh777

To get in touch with Caitlin please reach her at: caitlinleigh4@yahoo.com

Love and blessings and gratitude!

Made in the USA
Middletown, DE
10 April 2023